SCHIRMER'S LIBRARY
OF MUSICAL CLASSICS

New Edition

NICOLA VACCAI

Practical Method of Italian Singing

Edited,
with Introduction, Translation and Notes, by
JOHN GLENN PATON

G. SCHIRMER, Inc.

DISTRIBUTED BY
HAL•LEONARD®
CORPORATION
7777 W. BLUEMOUND RD. P.O. BOX 13819 MILWAUKEE, WI 53213

Introduction

Learning to sing means beginning an artistic journey full of rich and unexpected experiences. Human voices touch hearts in every nation and yet the best singing has qualities that Italy originated and taught the world to admire. Singing can approach a quality of timeless beauty, yet songs preserve for us the feelings of particular times, whether recent or long ago. Singing gives both singer and listener a sensation of freedom and heartfelt expression, yet it rests on a basis of disciplined practice and clear thinking.

Bel canto, beautiful singing, is the name we use today for the style of singing which Nicola Vaccai taught. You will see in this book what makes singers call it beautiful. Smooth, flowing melodies, supported by simple, harmonious accompaniments, flatter the voice and help it to become even, flexible, and expressive. Voices do not wear out from singing such music, rather they grow stronger, more beautiful, and more responsive to their owners' emotions.

When Vaccai's *Practical Method* appeared in London in 1833, a golden age of singing was in progress. Italian opera was fashionable and English society welcomed Italian visitors. One night at the opera a newspaper reporter saw in the audience the composers Bellini and Vaccai, the mezzo-soprano Giuditta Pasta, the tenor Rubini and the legendary violinist, Paganini. Other cities shared London's enthusiasm; even far away Mexico City and New York had heard Rossini's operas performed by the ambitious Garcia family. Singers, composers, and voice teachers were among Italy's most successful exports. In sunny Italy good voices abounded, and in the rich capitals of northern Europe many people would pay well to hear Italian singers or to take lessons from them.

Nicola Vaccai served a thorough musical apprenticeship at home before going abroad to seek honors and fortune. He was born in 1790 in Tolentino, near Ancona, but grew up in Pesaro, another town on the Adriatic seacoast. (A slightly younger Pesaro lad, Gioacchino Rossini, moved to Bologna at an early age; the two composers became friends years later.) Young Nicola studied music in Pesaro until his parents sent him to Rome to study law, the proper field for any young man who wanted a liberal education. Having no intention of becoming a lawyer, he took voice lessons and eventually studied counterpoint with Jannaconi, an important Roman composer. When Nicola turned twenty-one he went to Naples and became a disciple of Paisiello, whose *Barber of Seville* was considered a comic masterpiece until Rossini's *Barber* swept it from the stage a few years later.

After his first opera had a moderate beginner's success in Naples, Vaccai went to Venice for the production of his next two operas. For two decades he lived a nomadic life, spending months or years in Trieste, Vienna, Milan, Paris, wherever he was led by his double career of composition and teaching voice. Vaccai's sojourn in London began with a production of his most successful opera, *Romeo and Juliet,* at King's Theater in April, 1832. His personal charm and continental reputation ingratiated him to society and soon he was much sought after as a teacher.

Most voice teachers of that time worked in a slow and tedious way, aiming to perfect their pupils in scales, trills, and embellishments. Before a student was allowed to sing an aria he might spend years on solfeggi, exercises to be sung on "sol-fa" syllables or on pure vowels. Because Vaccai's English pupils were wealthy amateurs whose social position made a stage career unthinkable, he saw that a conventional rigorous training would only discourage them. For them he wrote tuneful exercises which they could sing with enjoyment while learning legato style, intervals, rhythms, the easier ornaments—in a word, musicianship. These short songs were published with the title *Metodo pratico di canto italiano per camera,* or *Practical Method of Italian Singing.* (The expression *per camera,* literally "for chamber," suggests training the voice for singing songs in contrast to training for the operatic theater.)

Ending his wandering with a return to Italy, Vaccai became director and professor of composition at the Milan Conservatory in 1838. After six years he retired on account of poor health to his boyhood home, Pesaro, where he wrote his sixteenth opera. He died in 1848, survived by a son, Giulio, who wrote his biography.

Vaccai's operas, which audiences enjoyed during his lifetime, were soon eclipsed by the more dramatic inspirations of Bellini and Donizetti and left behind by ever-changing operatic fashions. Ironically, the little exercise book which Vaccai wrote as a tool for his daily use became ever more popular and remains today an indispensable pedagogical work.

One novel feature of the *Practical Method* was the use of words in the exercises, for reasons which Vaccai explained in an introduction, "The Author's

Object." He chose the most elegant verses he knew, namely the texts of arias by Pietro Metastasio (1698-1782), a great poet whose specialty was writing opera librettos. Because copyright laws did not exist, Metastasio's poems could be set to music by anyone; for example, his *Alexander in India* had been used by seventy composers, including Gluck and Handel. Although no opera by Metastasio remains in today's standard repertoire, his complete librettos are still published in handsome editions for readers of Italian poetry.

By the 1830s Metastasio's stories of ancient heroes seemed pompous and dull, but the aria texts were still beautiful poems and Vaccai set them to music expressively and artistically in this book. Those who are ignorant of Italian say that we sing in that language only for the sake of its beautiful vowels, but the translations in this edition will show that Vaccai chose verses with distinct emotional values so that his pupils could learn to sing with expression. In some cases the words match Vaccai's musical purposes; for instance, a poem about conflict is used for the syncopation exercise and one about vacillating emotions is used for half-steps. If some of the meanings seem vague, one should try to imagine some dramatic situation in which a character would use a metaphor to communicate his feelings or would perhaps try to advise or persuade another person by means of a poetic image.

Practical Method has been continually in print since 1894 with G. Schirmer, Inc. This new edition removes many editorial alterations that represented turn-of-the-century performance practices and restores the authentic musical text of the earliest editions. The source used was a copy published in 1834 by T. Boosy & Co., London, and now owned by the British Museum. It contains Vaccai's preface and instructions in Italian and in English, anonymously translated. These translations appear here with their quaint orthography.

The poetic text has been altered in three ways: a few words have been corrected in keeping with recent scholarly editions of Metastasio; line-beginnings are shown by capital letters to help the singer grasp the form and rhyme of the poems; and certain pronunciation symbols are employed, as explained below in the article "Singing Italian."

Each Italian poem has been translated in two different ways. The literal translation at the bottom of each page will help the student who wants to sing in Italian with understanding. A singable version is also provided for the student who prefers to sing in English.

The notes at the back of the book result from my experiences in teaching the *Practical Method* to scores of students. I hope that, like almost every one of them, you will enjoy the smooth flow of your voice through Vaccai's graceful melodies.

Recalling Vaccai's remark that some aspects of singing can only be learned from "the voice of a skillful Master," I pay respect here to my teachers, Franklin Bens, Sonia Essin, and Julius Huehn, all participants in the great tradition of voice teaching.

John G. Paton
University of Colorado
Boulder, 1973

Singing Italian

VOWELS

Italian spelling is almost perfectly phonetic; that is, the letters tell us how to say the words. Our five vowel letters stand for fifteen different vowel sounds in English but only seven in Italian.

A resembles English *ah,* but is brighter, like the first sound (without a diphthong) in *aisle*

E has two sounds:

[ε], open, as in *set*

[e], closed and bright but not a diphthong, almost as in (French) *café*

I, except when silent as explained under "Consonants," is always closed and bright, as in *machine*

O has two sounds:

[ɔ], open, as in *ought*

[o], closed and dark but not a diphthong, as in *obey*

U is always closed and dark, as in *true,* but with a more open feeling inside the mouth.

In pronouncing unstressed syllables with *e* and *o,* Italian speakers use only the closed sounds, but singers often open them to [ε] and [ɔ]; the distinction is considered negligible because it does not affect the meaning. In stressed syllables with *e* and *o* the distinction between closed and open vowel sounds is essential, but there are no infallible rules to tell us which are which and they look alike in normal printing. In this book stressed closed vowels are printed in the ordinary way and stressed open vowels are distinguished by the phonetic symbols [ε] and [ɔ], for instance, lieve, pɔrto.

For good Italian vowels, remember:

1) Use lips and tongue vigorously to shape vowels;

2) Keep lips and tongue steady in one position during the whole time needed to say each vowel;

3) Keep the mouth open when a word ends in a vowel. Closing before the tone stops will produce an unwanted diphthong;

4) Some English vowel sounds never occur in Italian. Be alert so that these vowels do not intrude accidentally into your Italian: *sit* [ɪ]; *sat* [æ]; *sun* [ʌ]; *put* [ʊ]; *turn* [ɜ]; and the last vowel in *sofa* [ə].

DIPHTHONGS

When two vowels are combined in one syllable to form a diphthong, one vowel is pronounced as quickly as possible and the other, called the syllabic vowel, is lengthened to fill out the duration of the sung tone. In English diphthongs (for instance, *now*) the syllabic vowel is always the first one, but in Italian it may be either. In this book the syllabic vowel is underlined: mio, sua, più, uɔmo.

Diphthongs also occur in connected speech or song when one word ends in a vowel and the next begins with a vowel. The two, sometimes three or four, vowels combine smoothly into one syllable with the syllabic vowel shown thus: "Presso al"; "vede il"; "lido, e il."

Be sure that all the vowels on one note are sung cleanly on pitch; a common error is to sing a short vowel as if it were a grace note on a different pitch from the syllabic vowel.

CONSONANTS

Italian consonants tend to be softer than ours; accentuation and emphasis are accomplished in Italian through the vowels. No Italian consonant explodes with a puff of air such as we use for *k, p,* and *t.* Italian consonants are formed as far forward in the mouth as possible; the tongue should actually touch the upper teeth in pronouncing *d, n, t,* and *l.* Otherwise, these consonants are identical in English and Italian: *B, D, F, L, M, P, T,* and *V.*

Some consonants need special attention, especially *C, G,* and *SC,* which have a "soft" sound when followed by *e* or *i* and a "hard" sound when followed by any other letter.

C before *e* or *i* is pronounced [tʃ], as in *violoncello*

C otherwise is pronounced [k], as in *cow*

G before *e* or *i* is pronounced [dʒ], as in *gem*

G otherwise is pronounced [g], as in *go*

SC before *e* or *i* is pronounced [ʃ], as in *luscious*

SC otherwise is pronounced [sk], as in *scale*

If the hard sound is desired before *e* or *i,* a silent *h* is added, as in *orchestra, spaghetti, scherzo.* If the soft sound is desired before *a, o,* or *u,* a silent letter *i* is inserted, as in *Giovanni, ciao, lascia.* (Note that *i,* used in this fashion, and *h* are the only silent letters in Italian; all others must be pronounced.)

H is always silent.

N is usually pronounced as in *no*

N before hard *c* or hard *g* becomes [ŋ], as in *anchor* or *angry*

QU is pronounced [kw], as in *queen*

R is always flipped or rolled with the tip of the tongue.

S is usually pronounced as in *lasso*

S when single between two vowels is pronounced [z], as in *rose*

S before a voiced consonant is pronounced [z], as in *wisdom*

Z is usually pronounced [ts], as in *pizza*

In some words [dz] is preferred, for instance, *mezzo.*

Two Italian consonant sounds are foreign to English but very easy.

GLI: Say "all ye," and feel the tip of your tongue strike the roof of the mouth. Now place the tip of the tongue behind the lower teeth and try to say "all ye"; instead you say an Italian word, *agli* ['aʎi]. [ʎ] is always spelled *gli*; in *agli* the *i* is syllabic, but before another vowel the *i* may be silent, as in *periglio* [pe 'riʎo].

GN: Say "own ye," and feel the tip of your tongue strike the roof of the mouth. Now place the tip of the tongue behind the lower teeth and try to say "own ye" with a pure [o]; you will have said an Italian word, *ogni* ['oɲi]. [ɲ] is spelled *gn,* no matter what vowel follows.

To review, notice that in saying *palio* ['palio] the tip of the tongue touches the roof of the mouth, but in *paglia* ['paʎa] it stays behind the lower teeth. In saying *niego* ['niɛgo] the tip of the tongue touches the roof of the mouth, but in *igneo* ['iʎeo] it stays behind the lower teeth.

Our alphabet has five letters that Italian does not: *J, K, W, X,* and *Y.* Formerly, *j* was considered a form of *i* and was used for the weaker vowel in a diphthong. In his day the composer's name would be spelled Vaccaj. Today it is spelled Vaccai.

English has five consonant sounds that Italian does not: *hat* [h]; *what* [hw]; *thin* [θ]; *this* [ð]; and *vision* [ʒ].

DOUBLE CONSONANTS

Italian has true double consonants, which must be pronounced correctly for correct meanings. For example, the aria *Una furtiva lagrima* from Donizetti's "L'Elisir d'Amore" contains the words, *"M'ama, si, m'ama,"* "She loves me, yes, she loves me." If the tenor sings double *mm's* by mistake, he seems to be calling for "Mamma."

Double consonants take more than twice as much time as single ones, whether they are sustained, like *mm* or *rr,* or stopped, like *bb* or *tt.* Doubling does not affect the quality of a consonant, except that *ss* remains [s], not [z], between vowels.

The first of a pair of consonants belongs to the preceding syllable and note, the second to the following syllable and note. When soft c is doubled, the preceding syllable stops with [t] and the following syllable begins with [tʃ]. When soft g is doubled, [d] is the stop-consonant.

For more detailed information and a wealth of examples, the student should consult *Singers' Italian* by Evelina Colorni, G. Schirmer, Inc., 1970.

For help with English, the student should consult *The Singer's Manual of English Diction* by Madeleine Marshall, G. Schirmer, Inc.

The Author's Object in This Practical Method

There can be no doubt that Italian singing, in consequence of the peculiar advantages it owes to the Language, is the best for those to begin with, who are desirous of attaining considerable proficiency in the art; for when once they have mastered the difficulties of this style, it will be easy for them to sing in any language with which they are acquainted: an advantage that would not be gained by beginning with any other than Italian singing. Having found by long experience (in Germany, in France, in England, and, I may add, even in Italy) that most, if not all, of those who learn merely for amusement, are averse to occupying their time with long Solfeggi and other Exercises: affirming that their only object being to sing in private society, they are unwilling to go through the drudgery of the usual systems: I devised the method which I here present to the Public, quite new in its kind, short, amusing, and useful, and by means of which, the end proposed may be attained with equal certainty, and in less time.

But as the great difficulty for Foreigners, lies in the articulation, and correct pronunciation of the Italian words; a difficulty that is not removed by the longest course of Solfeggi, and of Exercises sung to a vowel sound: I conceived, that even from the first scale exercises, it would be a better plan to accustom the learner to pronounce the language itself, rather than confine him to syllables devoid of meaning.* I therefore selected from among the beautiful Poems of Metastasio, those which I judged best suited to my purpose, and have made use of them, to render, I hope, less irksome those first rules, to the *taedium* of learning which, no one seems disposed to submit.

I am persuaded that this new method will prove most useful, not only to Amateurs, but also to those who dedicate themselves to singing as a profession; in as much as the practical nature and application of the examples, will make it serve as a sort of developement and demonstration to every other System.

On the compass of the Voice.

In every example in this work I have confined myself to a limited compass of voice, not only for the greater convenience of voices in general, but because it is better, in the beginning, to exercise chiefly the centre or middle notes of the voice, always quite sufficient for the purpose of learning all the necessary rules. On the other hand, there will be no difficulty in transposing any one or more of the Lessons, if found requisite.

---

*For those who are learning the rudiments of Music and Singing *at the same time,* it will be useful no doubt to begin with the musical monosyllables, but this practice can never teach the true Syllabication or manner of dividing the Syllables and uniting them to the notes, since it affords no practical illustration of the Elision of the Vowels, nor of the other peculiarities which are treated of in the first Lesson.

LESSON I
La Scala — The Scale

The manner of dividing the Syllables in this first lesson, will be found to differ altogether from the ordinary orthographical Syllabication; in order to give, as far as possible, an idea of the right manner of pronouncing in Singing, and to indicate how one should expend the whole value of one or more notes on the *vowel* of the Syllable, uniting its *consonant* to the next Syllable following; by this practice also the Pupil will gradually be taught to sing *Legato* — an art however, which nothing but the voice of a skillful Master can communicate perfectly to the learner.

Literal translation: [The flame] fails rapidly,/ more than usual,/ even if it flickers/ with a light breath,/ the flame that sputters./ close to dying.

Salti di Terza — Intervals of Thirds *

*The term *Interval* (the *difference* between two notes) is not strictly the equivalent of *Salto* (the *Skip* from one note to another) but is adopted here, as being the expression in common use.

N.V.

The silly turtledove,/ that does not see its danger,/[in order]to flee from the cruel talon [of a falcon]/ flies into the lap of the hunter.

[He] leaves the shore,/ and the treacherous sea/ to plow returns the steersman,/ and yet he knows that, deceitful,/ other times it cheated him.

47364

Salti di Quinta — Intervals of Fifths

Accustomed to living/ without comfort,/ again in the harbor/ you fear the sea.

LESSON III
Salti di Sesta — Intervals of Sixths

Beautiful proof is [this] of a strong soul: / being placid and serene/ in suffering the unjust pain/ of a guilt that [one does] not have.

LESSON IV
Salti di Settima — Intervals of Sevenths

In darkness one lightning-flash alone / suffices for the wise steersman, / who already rediscovers the [direction of the north] pole, / already recognizes [where he is on] the sea.

Vaccai omitted the second line of the poem, "Dalla pendice alpina." The complete translation is: That wave that rushes headlong/ from the mountainous hillside/ leaps, breaks, and murmurs,/ but makes itself clear.

LESSON V
I Semitoni — The Semitones

[Every soul] wanders doubtfully, / uncertainly raves, / every soul that wavers / between emotions of the heart.

LESSON VI
Modo Sincopato — Syncopation

In strife Cupid is inflamed: / with one who surrenders, to one who yields, / never so cruel is he.

LESSON VII
Introduzione alle Volate
Preparatory Example for the Roulade

This lesson must be sung *Adagio* at first, and the time accelerated to *Allegro*, according to the ability of the Pupil.

Like the whiteness/ of untouched snow/ is of a good heart/ the faithfulness:/ one mark only/ that it receives/ completely from it steals/ its beauty.

47364

14

LESSON VIII
Le Appoggiature sopra, e sotto
Appoggiaturas above and below

The Appoggiatura is the best ornament made use of in Singing; its effect depends mainly upon giving the appoggiatural note its precise value. It is however not so much a fault to *add* to the appoggiatura as to abstract from its value.

N.V.

Without the lovable/ god from Cythera (Cupid)/ the days do not return/ of spring./ a breeze does not blow,/ a flower does not peep out./ The grass on the edge/ of the friendly spring,/ the leafless plants/ on the sunny hill,/ for him restore/ the old adornment.

47364

L'Acciaccatura — The Acciaccatura

The Acciaccatura differs from the Appoggiatura in as much as it does not interfere with the value or the accent of the note to which it is prefixed.

Although of speech deprived,/ the slim young tree is grateful/ to that friendly stream/ from which it receives moisture./ By it with leafy branches adorned,/ a beautiful mercy it renders,/ when from the sun it defends/ its benefactor.

17

47364

LESSON IX
Introduzione al Mordente — Preparatory Example for the Mordent

The Mordente is the ornament which offers the greatest variety, as well as the greatest difficulty in its execution, on account of the lightness and neatness which it requires. It consists of two, or three notes, and adds much to the grace of the Phrase, without taking any thing away, or interfering at all with the intention of the Composer. And here it may be to the purpose to observe, that all those alterations which People are in the habit of making in Singing, (and which, by a singular abuse of terms, are called embellishments,) whenever they disfigure the original melody, or interfere with the accent intended by the Author, are out of place, faulty, and bad.

N.V.

True joy,/ to make itself known,/ of a talkative mouth/ has no need.

gio - ia __ ve - ra - ce. Per far - si __ pa - le - se, D'un

heart __ tru - ly __ hap-py Will find __ free __ ex - pres-sion. It

lab - bro lo - qua - ce Bi - so - gno non __

needs __ no con - fes - sion To __ make __ it - self __

ha. No, no, __ no, __ no, __ no, __ no, __ bi - so - gno __ non __ ha.

known. No, no, __ no, __ no, __ no, __ no, To __ make __ it - self __ known.

Il Medesimo in diversi modi — The same exemplified in various ways

The little bird in a narrow cage,/ why does one never hear it sing?/ Because it hopes some time/ to return to liberty.

LESSON X
Introduzione al Gruppetto — Preparatory Example for the Turn

In this Lesson, the same rule as suggested for the Seventh Lesson should be attended to.

N.V.

Quan – do ac – cen – de un__ no – bil__ pɛt – to,

In a ____ no – ble ____ heart's de – vo – tion

ɛ in – no – cen – te e ___ pu – ro af – fɛt – to: De – bo –

Burns a ____ strong and ____ pure e – mo – tion: It's not ___

lez – za a – mor non ___ ɛ. Quan – do ac – cen – de un

weak – ness to be in ___ love. In ___ a ___ no – ble

When inflames a noble breast, / it is innocent and pure emotion: / love is not weakness.

47364

no - bil pɛt - to, è in - no - cɛn - te e pu - ro af -

heart's — de - vo - tion Burns — a — strong — and a pure, — pure e -

fɛt-to: De - bo - lez - za a - mor — non — è,

mo-tion: It's — not — weak - ness to — be in — love,

De - bo - lez - za a - mor — non è.

It's — not weak - ness to — be — in love.

Il Gruppetto — The Turn

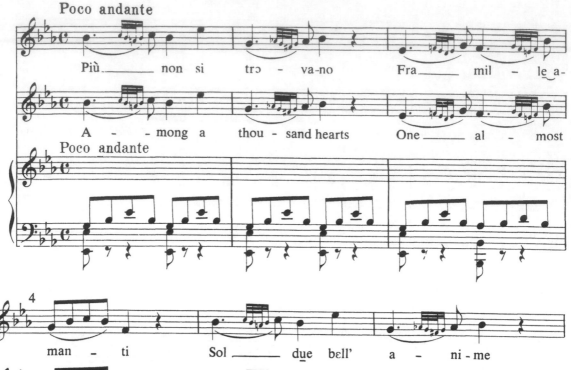

No longer does one find/ among a thousand lovers/ even two good souls/ that are constant,/ and everybody speaks of faithfulness.

LESSON XI
Introduzione al Trillo — Preparatory Example for the Shake

Se po-ve - ro il ru - scel - lo

The brook through—mead-ows mur — murs

Mor-mo - ra_ len-to_e bas - so, Un ra-mo - scel - lo, un

So qui - et - ly and so——lone, As if one—— twig-let, one

sas - so Qua - si ar - res-tar__ lo__ fa. Se

small——stone, Could make it al - most__ stop. The

If the poor brook / murmurs slowly and low, / a twig, a pebble, / seems to arrest it.

LESSON XII
Le Volate — On Roulades

We are ships on the frigid waves / left in abandonment: / impetuous winds / our emotions are; / every delight is a rock; / all life is sea.

O - gni di - let - to è sco - glio: Tut - ta la vi - ta è

Pleas - ures are on - ly dan - gers: All of our life is a

mar, O - gni di - let - to è sco - glio: Tut - ta la

sea, Pleas - ures are on - ly dan - gers, All of our

vi - ta è mar, Tut - ta la vi - ta è un mar.

life is a sea, All of our life is but a sea.

LESSON XIII
Modo per portare la voce
On the Glide or manner of carrying the Voice

By carrying the voice from one note to another, it is not meant that you should drag or drawl the voice through all the intermediate intervals, an abuse that is frequently committed — but it means, to *unite* perfectly, the one note with the other. When once the Pupil understands thoroughly how to unite the Syllables, as pointed out in the first Lesson, he will more easily learn the manner of carrying the voice as here intended: of this however, as before observed, nothing but the voice of an able Master can give a perfectly clear notion. There are two ways of carrying the voice. The first is, by *anticipating* as it were almost insensibly, with the *vowel* of the preceding Syllable, the note you are about to take, as shewn in the first example. In phrases requiring much grace and expression, it produces a very good effect: the abuse of it, however, is to be carefully avoided, as it leads to Mannerism and Monotony.

The other method, which is less in use, is by *deferring* or *postponing* as it were almost insensibly the note you are going to take, and pronouncing the Syllable that belongs to it, with the note you are leaving, as pointed out in the Second example.

I would explain my anguish, / I would hide it; / and meanwhile my doubts / thus are growing. / All to explain I dare not, /

13

Tut - to non so ___ ta - cer, Tut-to spie- gar, tut - to ___ non so, non so ta-

Do ___ I dare hold ___ my peace? Do I dare speak, or ___ do ___ I dare to ___ hold my

rf *p*

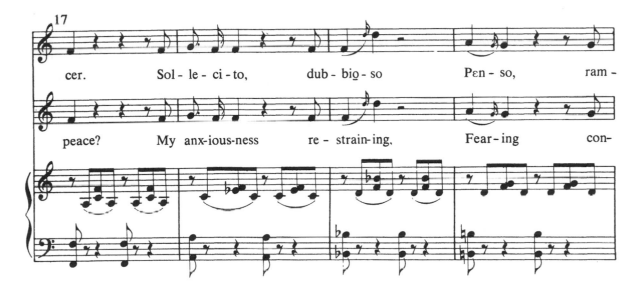

17

cer. Sol - le - ci - to, dub - bio - so Pen - so, ram -

peace? My anx-ious-ness re - strain-ing, Fear-ing con-

21

men - to, ram-men-to ___ e ve - do; E a-gli oc-chi ___ miei non

fes - sion, yet scorn-ing pre - tens-es, I ___ can - not ___ trust my ___

I can not keep silent about everything./ Anxious, doubtful;/ I think, I remember, and I see,/ and I can not
believe my eyes,/

47364

I can not believe my thoughts.

Altro Modo —- The other Method

Whether the placid sea/ gleams on the beach,/ or carries with the wave/ terror and fright,/ it is the fault of the wind,/ its own fault it is not.

LESSON XIV
Il Recitativo — On Recitative

Recitative requires a distinct and marked Syllabication, nor can it ever prove effective without a perfect accentuation. When two notes of the same name and value occur at the *end* of a Period, or even when several similar notes occur in the *middle* of a period, the note, on which the accent of the Word falls becomes altogether an Appoggiatura to the following note. To make this perfectly clear, the note, on which the accented Syllable falls, is marked with the letter *a* over it.

The homeland is a whole, of which we are parts. A citizen is wrong to consider himself separated from her. The only profit or gain that he ought to know is that which benefits or hurts his homeland, to which he is in debt for everything.

When sweat or blood he sheds for her, nothing of his own he gives: he renders only that which from her he had. She produced him, reared him, fed him: with her laws from domestic injury defends him, from foreign, with arms.

36

She gives him name, rank, and honor, rewards his merit, avenges his offenses, and, a loving mother, she exerts herself to fashion his happiness, inasmuch as it is granted to the destiny of mortals to be happy.

47364

Riepilogo — Recapitulation

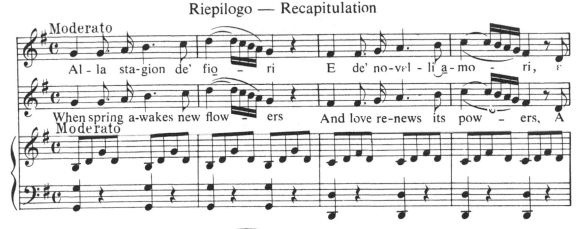

In the season of flowers / and of new loves / pleasant is the delicate breath of a zephyr light. / Whether it moans among the branches / or slowly ripples the waves, / Zephyrus everywhere / the comrade is of pleasure.

38

ge - ma, o ge - ma tra__ le fron - de, O len - to, o
sigh-ing, if sigh - ing fills__ the ce - dars, Or gent-ly, or

len - to, o len - to in - cre - spi__ l'on - de,
gent-ly, or gen - tly__ rip - ples__ riv - ers,

Ze - fi - ro in o - gni la - to Com - pa - gno è del pia-
Zeph-y-rus sighs all a - round us, Con - vey - ing thoughts of

Notes by the Editor

Page 3. Vaccai printed the first two texts so that each syllable appears to end with a vowel. He did this because vowels are prolonged in singing, and a consonant which occurs at the end of a syllable is attached to the beginning of the next syllable. If we did the same in English, our text would read: "Whe- na-ny ca- nde-lfla- me . . ." Conventionally printed, the Italian poem reads:

> Manca sollecita
> Più dell'usato,
> Ancor che s'agiti
> Con lieve fiato,
> Face che palpita
> Presso al morir.

Vaccai surely chose this melancholy verse for his first lesson because it contains the words *con lieve fiato,* "with light breath." These words recall the singing teacher's classic trick of holding a lighted candle in front of a student's mouth, close enough so that puffs of uncontrolled breath make the flame waver. Only by managing the use of his breath carefully will the student succeed in singing these slow scales. Although it is at the beginning of the book, this exercise is one of the most difficult. The student should expect to study it for a few weeks, then put it away and return to it later.

Page 4. This melody shows Vaccai's preference for rhythmic lightness and grace in that every phrase begins on an upbeat and most phrases have feminine endings. The poem reads:

> Semplicetta tortorella,
> Che non vede il suo periglio,
> Per fuggir dal crudo artiglio,
> Vola in grembo al cacciator.

Page 12. Here are some interesting examples of Italian freedom in the musical treatment of diphthongs. The two syllables, *-de, a,* share one note in m. 6, but have two notes in m. 18. In m. 25 *mai* is printed as one syllable and the singer should slur downward on the vowel [a]. But in the first edition m. 21 had no slur and *mai* was printed in two syllables, *ma-i.* Apparently both ways of singing this word were considered acceptable.

Page 14. Beginning here, we will study the bel canto "ornaments," which are not useless decorations, but technical devices used by all composers of the time. Certain ornaments require flexibility and speed but others are easy to sing if only we understand the appropriate musical notation. Appoggiaturas belong to the latter group.

Appoggiare means "to lean," and an appoggiatura is a way of approaching a note slantwise, so to speak, by way of its neighboring note. Appoggiaturas are not the rapid grace-notes that every piano student plays; those are acciaccaturas, taken up in the next exercise.

Appoggiaturas occur on strong beats and last for measurable lengths of time. Composers were often careless about showing these durations, but Vaccai was precise: in m. 2 the appoggiatura should last one beat and, as a result, the next quarter-note is shortened to an eighth. According to Vaccai's instructions a sixteenth-note appoggiatura would be wrong here, but it would not be a serious error to lengthen the appoggiatura to a dotted eighth or perhaps even to a quarter, completely replacing the printed quarter-note. Notice that in some cases the appoggiatura and the main note are the same length, so that if the appoggiatura is sung at all, the main note must be omitted.

Why didn't Vaccai write the notes he wanted to hear? First, for centuries there had been a traditional prohibition against writing dissonances on strong beats; one way of evading this rule was by writing the dissonant note smaller and close beside a consonant one. Earlier composers also had a practical reason, namely, that most music was handwritten, difficult to read, and full of mistakes. An eighteenth-century accompanist normally had only the melody and bass notes in his score, and from them he had to deduce what chords he should play. Obviously, having nonchordal notes in the melody might mislead him so that he would play incorrect chords.

Are appoggiaturas weak and unimportant because they are small? To answer this for yourself, sing through the exercise without any appoggiaturas, and since everything will be consonant, the piece will sound bland and unexpressive. We notice also that Vaccai used appoggiaturas on strong beats and on strong syllables of important words; apparently he meant them to be expressive, indeed more important than other notes, despite their small printed size.

Page 16. According to Vaccai's description, the acciaccatura must be very quick and before the beat in this music although that may not be true for earlier periods of music. Literally a "crushed" note, the acciaccatura, also sometimes referred to as a "short appoggiatura," is shown in most modern editions by a small note with a diagonal line through its stem. Vaccai did not use this method, but expected singers to learn to distinguish long appoggiaturas from short acciaccaturas by knowing certain customary rules. One was that a small note was to be sung as an acciaccatura if the following normal-sized note was nonharmonic; this is the case throughout Lesson VIIIB. Studying music of this era, one quickly learns that composers were inconsistent about distinctions between ornaments, probably because they expected singers to have enough training and initiative to make such small decisions for themselves.

Page 18. *Mordente* means "biting." Pianists know that a mordent gives "bite" to the beginning of a note and that it consists of the written note and its lower neighbor quickly alternated. Vaccai's mordent is something entirely different, one not found in musical dictionaries: a graceful means of leaving a note by feinting upwards when the next melodic note is downwards, or vice versa.

Despite Vaccai's stern warning against tasteless distortions of the music, he did not absolutely forbid his students to embellish their songs. He seems to say that there are better and worse ways to embellish and that the mordent offers a way that could not possibly offend anyone.

Page 20. Here Vaccai gives an extremely plain melody sixteen measures long and then shows in the next sixteen measures how this melody could be embellished by the tasteful use of varied mordents. He is preparing his students to improvise ornamentation as great singers of that time were expected to do. (The accidentals in the voice part of mm. 19 and 27 did not appear in the first edition, but they seem reasonable.)

Page 22. The ornamental notes in mm. 9, 11, and 15 are appoggiaturas. In each case sing four equal sixteenth-notes.

Page 24. *Gruppetto* means a "little group" of five notes always in this order: main note, upper neighbor, main note, lower neighbor, and main note. All notes except the first are printed small and time in which to sing them must be stolen from other notes. Two solutions to this problem are offered here, with the more complex one in m. 1: instead of a dotted quarter-note, sing a quarter tied to a 32nd and three more 32nds, and instead of the eighth-note, sing two sixteenths. Thus, five notes fit into the time allotted for two.

Written: Sung:

Più _____ non   Più _____ non

The simpler pattern appears in m. 7: the quarter-note should be sung as an eighth and the other notes as 32nds.

Written: Sung:

che _____   che _____

Notice that at the end of m. 3 the diphthong *"le a"* must be sung on a sixteenth because the eighth has lost part of its value following the turn.

Written: Sung:

mil - - le a   mil - - le a

Page 26. "Shake" and "trill" mean the same in England, but in America we use only the latter word. Most students expect trills to be difficult but this exercise leads easily to a true measured trill in m. 20. Vaccai's trills are accented on the upper note, as they should be for Bach, Mozart, and all eighteenth-century composers.

Page 34. Recitatives are used in opera and oratorio to carry the story-line and to prepare the emotional situations in which characters are moved to sing arias. Recitatives present certain problems, including: learning nonrepetitive rhythms; grasping key changes, often ahead of the chords that will establish new keys; clear diction; vocal tone that is beautiful, yet similar to a speaking voice in quality; subtlety in phrasing so that the words sound natural without departing too far from the musical notation; the use of appoggiaturas. For the reasons mentioned with regard to Lesson VIII only chord-tones were written on strong beats in recitatives, but every composer expected that singers would know this rule: if two consecutive notes have the same length and pitch and the first of them is accented, that note may be sung one scale-step higher than written. In this case the written pitch is not sung at all but completely replaced by the appoggiatura. Notice also that one must know what scale is in use at each moment; for instance, in m. 23 the appoggiatura must be flatted, but in m. 24, second beat, the appoggiatura is not flatted because the key has changed in that short time. The student who patiently works out this exercise will have no problem with any operatic recitative.

Page 37. In m. 7 the small sixteenth-notes are sung as acciaccaturas because each precedes the first of a group of equal, quick notes.